FATHERS AND SONS

Borgo Press Dramas by FRANK J. MORLOCK

Chuzzlewit
Crime and Punishment
Falstaff (with William Shakespeare, John Dennis, and William Kendrick)
Fathers and Sons
Notes from the Underground
Outrageous Women: Lady Macbeth and Other French Plays (editor and translator)
A Raw Youth
The Stendhal Hamlet Scenarios and Other Shakespearean Shorts from the French (editor and translator)

FATHERS AND SONS

A PLAY IN FIVE ACTS

FRANK J. MORLOCK

Adapted from the Novel by Ivan Turgenev

THE BORGO PRESS
MMXII

FATHERS AND SONS

Copyright © 1982, 2012 by Frank J. Morlock

FIRST BORGO PRESS EDITION

Published by Wildside Press LLC

www.wildsidebooks.com

DEDICATION

To the memory of my father,

Michael Morlock;

And to my uncle,

Paris Pierson

CONTENTS

CAST OF CHARACTERS	9
ACT I, Scene 1	11
ACT I, Scene 2	34
ACT I, Scene 3	44
ACT II, Scene 4	53
ACT II, Scene 5	61
ACT III, Scene 6	78
ACT III, Scene 7	89
ACT IV, Scene 8	110
ACT IV, Scene 9	123
ACT IV, Scene 10	136
ACT IV, Scene 11	144
ACT V, Scene 12	163
ACT V, Scene 13	172
ACT V, Scene 14	178
ABOUT THE AUTHOR	185

CAST OF CHARACTERS

Piotr

Nicolai Petrovitch Kirsanov

Arkady Kirsanov

Eugeny Bazarov

Dunyasha

Pavel Petrovitch Kirsanov

Fenitchka

Peasant Boy

Anna Sergeyevna Odinstov

Katya, her sister

Old Bazarov

Madame Bazarov

Servant

German Doctor

The play is set circa 1860 in rural Russia.

ACT I
SCENE 1

The garden of Nicolai Kirsanov's estate. On the right a porch. Piotr is on a ladder watching the road. To the left a swing set in an artificial bower.

Nicolai

Well, Piotr, not in sight yet?

Piotr

No, Sir, not in sight.

Nicolai

Not in sight?

Piotr

No, Sir.

Nicolai (sighs)

They should be here.

Piotr

The coach is always late.

Nicolai

Of course.

(Piotr comes down from the ladder)

Piotr

Good thing this doesn't happen often. I'm too old to be climbing about on ladders. What if I fell?

Nicolai

You're as agile as a cat.

Piotr

All the same. It's no way to treat a servant.

Nicolai

Just once I ask you and you complain.

Piotr

One is free now. Not a serf any more. It is permitted to complain.

Nicolai

But must you make a profession of it?

Piotr

Freedom is freedom. What good is it if one can't express oneself?

(A noise offstage)

It sounds as if they're coming, Sir.

Nicolai

Arkasha, Arkasha.

(Arkady and Bazarov enter)

Arkady

Let me shake myself first, Daddy. I will cover you with dust.

Nicolai (not noticing Bazarov)

Never mind, never mind. Let me have a look at you; let me have a look at you.

Arkady

Daddy, let me introduce you to my great friend, Bazarov, about whom I have so often written to you. He has been so good as to promise to stay with us.

Nicolai

I am heartily glad and very grateful for your kind intention of visiting us. Let me know your name and your father's—

Bazarov

Eugeny Vassilyitch.

Nicolai

I hope, dear Eugeny Vassilyitch, you won't find it dull with us.

(To Piotr)

Please see to Mr. Bazarov's things, Piotr. Give him the room next to Arkady's.

Piotr

Will you please accompany me, Sir?

(Bazarov exits into the house with Piotr)

Nicolai

So here you are, a graduate at last, and come home again. At last.

Arkady

And how is Uncle?

Nicolai

Quite well. He was going to wait with me but for some reason or other changed his mind. I think he knew I should want to have you all to myself for a bit.

Arkady

And, how long have you been waiting for me?

Nicolai

Oh, about five hours.

Arkady

Dear, old Dad!

(Arkady kisses his father on the cheek)

Nicolai

I have got a capital horse for you. You will see. And your room has been fresh papered.

Arkady

Is there a room for Bazarov?

Nicolai

Of course.

Arkady

Please Dad, make much of him. I can't tell you how I prize his friendship.

Nicolai

Have you made friends with him lately?

Arkady

Yes, quite lately.

Nicolai

Ah, that accounts for my not seeing him last winter.

(Pause)

What does he study?

Arkady

Natural science. But he knows everything. Next year he'll take his doctor's degree.

Nicolai

Ah,—a physician. That's good. Russia can use doctors. Incidentally, Arkady, I've had a lot of bother with the peasants this year.

Arkady

Now that they've been emancipated. They're difficult, eh?

Nicolai

Yes. They are being set against me.

Arkady (examining the garden)

You've no shade; it's a pity.

Nicolai

But I've had an awning put up—

(He points)

We can have dinner even in the open air.

Arkady

What air though? I don't believe there's such a fragrance in the world as in the meadows here.

(Arkady is suddenly embarrassed by his own enthusiasm)

What would Bazarov say if he heard me gushing like this?

Nicolai

Of course. You were born here, so everything here is special to you.

Arkady

Oh, Dad, it makes no difference where a man was born.

Nicolai

Still—

Arkady

No. It makes absolutely no difference.

Nicolai (pause)

I don't recollect whether I told you but your old nurse, Yegorovura, is dead.

Arkady

Really? Poor thing!

Nicolai

That's about the only change here at Margino.

Arkady

That suits me fine.

Nicolai

Ah.

(Hesitates)

There is one change. I think it my duty to prepare you.

(Pause)

A severe moralist might regard my openness as improper; but after all it can't be concealed—

(Nicolai is having hard going)

Of course, I have always had decided ideas about the relation of father and son— What I mean is—you have a right to disapprove, of course, however—

(He is helpless)

Arkady (easily)

Fenitchka?

Nicolai (mortified)

Don't mention her name aloud, please.

(Pause)

Well, she is living with me now. I have installed her in the house—in two little rooms off the drawing room.

(Pause)

But that can all be changed.

Arkady

(who is somewhat amused at his father's embarrassment)

Goodness, Daddy, what for?

Nicolai

Your friend is going to stay with us—it would be awkward. Not to mention your legitimate objections.

Arkady

Please don't be uneasy on my account or Bazarov's. He's above all that.

Nicolai

Well, but, you, too—the little cabin is so horrid—that's the worst of it.

Arkady

Goodness, Dad, it's as if you were apologizing. You act as if you're ashamed.

Nicolai (terribly embarrassed)

Of course, I'm ashamed.

Arkady

Nonsense, Dad, nonsense; please don't. What a thing to apologize for! Please, stop—

Nicolai (changing the subject)

I have sold the timber.

Arkady

Why?

Nicolai

The money was needed.

Arkady

I'm sorry about the timber. But what an exquisite day it is today!

Nicolai

To welcome you, my dear boy. Anyway, now you are at home, we must have supper and rest.

(Bazarov returning with Piotr)

Bazarov

A meal would not come amiss, certainly.

Nicolai

Yes, yes, let us have supper directly.

Piotr

You wish supper to be served?

Nicolai

Yes, yes—

Piotr

The cook has been ready for Arkady. It will only be a minute.

Nicolai

Wouldn't you like to change, Arkady?

Arkady

No thanks. But, I'd better wash up.

Bazarov

Arkady, have you got a light?

(He brandishes his pipe)

Arkady

Of course.

Bazarov

Will you have a cigar?

Arkady

Cigarette, I think, thanks.

(Enter Pavel Petrovitch, a man of about forty-five. Elegantly dressed after an English style. He is in a dark English suit, a fashionable low cravat and kid shoes. He is aristocratic, elegant, graceful. He has exquisitely manicured hands.)

Pavel

Welcome, Arkady. I had begun to think you were not coming.

(He kisses Arkady three times in the Russian manner)

Arkady

I am fine, Uncle Paul. We had a slight delay. You must meet Bazarov.

(Pavel turns politely to Bazarov and makes a little bow. His aesthetic reaction to Bazarov is instantaneously hostile, although he is too polished a gentleman to be rude.)

(Pavel greets Bazarov with a slight inclination of his supple figure. Bazarov responds with a somewhat exaggerated bow which may be due to awkwardness but possibly to satire.)

Pavel

Charmed, I'm sure.

Arkady

Tell Piotr to hurry up. We're hungry as wolves. I'm going to wash up. I'll be back directly.

Bazarov

I'm coming with you.

(Bazarov and Arkady exit into the house)

Pavel

Who is he?

Nicolai

A friend of Arkady's. A very clever fellow.

Pavel

Is he going to stay with us?

Nicolai

Yes.

Pavel

That unkempt creature?

(Piotr enters from the house with a large tray of food which he places on the table under the awning)

Piotr

Dinner is served.

(Bazarov and Arkady return)

Nicolai

That was quick.

Bazarov

We smelled food.

(They all sit down at the table, a servant girl comes in)

Little Girl

Fedosya Nikolaevna is not quite well; she cannot come. Will you please pour tea yourself or should she send Dunyasha?

Nicolai

I will pour for myself, then. Arkady, how do you take your tea—with cream or with lemon?

Arkady

With cream.

(Pause)

Daddy.

Nicolai

Well?

(Nicolai senses what is coming and he is mortified)

Arkady

Is the reason Fenitchka will not come to pour tea because I'm here?

Nicolai (turning away to hide his confusion)

Perhaps—she is embarrassed.

Arkady

She has no reason to be embarrassed. You know my views. If you have chosen her to live with you—she must be worthy of it.

Nicolai (profoundly moved)

Thanks, Arkasha. Of course, it's not some—some caprice, or a cheap affair. It's not easy for me to talk to you about this. But, you understand it's difficult for her—especially the first day—of your return.

Arkady (rising)

In that case I will go to her. I will fix everything.

Nicolai (completely disconcerted)

But, Arkady—you can't. I haven't told you yet— My God—

(But Arkady has gone)

Pavel

He doesn't know about the child?

Nicolai

Whatever will happen?

Bazarov

Trust Arkady to do the right thing.

(Bazarov has been eating unconcernedly throughout this conversation)

Nicolai

Oh, of course. I'm sorry, Mr. Bazarov, to expose you to such— intimate family scenes.

Bazarov

Think nothing of it.

Pavel (guarded but polite)

I have been trying to remember where I heard your name before. Was your father a military surgeon, Mr. Bazarov?

Bazarov

My father and my grandfather were in the horse guards.

Pavel

Ah, I remember your grandfather, he died a hero's death at Sebastopol.

Bazarov

He died like a fool, in a foolish war.

Pavel

That is a rather harsh way to speak of one's grandfather.

Bazarov

As he is my grandfather, I feel I have the right to take that liberty. My grandfather was a romantic. So, for that matter, is my father.

Pavel

You seem to have little respect for received opinions.

Bazarov

That is true. I am a nihilist.

Pavel

Eh?

Bazarov

A nihilist.

Nicolai (nonchalantly munching)

A nihilist, that from the Latin—nihil—nothing. The word must mean a man who accepts nothing—

Pavel

Who respects nothing—

Bazarov

Who regards everything from a critical point of view.

Pavel

Isn't that just the same?

Bazarov

No,—a nihilist is a man who does not bow down before any authority regardless of what reverence attaches to it.

Pavel

A sort of revolutionary par excellence, eh?

(Bazarov nods and munches)

Pavel

Indeed. Well, it's not in our line. We are old-fashioned folk. We think that without principles, taken as you say on faith, there's no taking a step, no breathing. Vous avez change tout cela.

Bazarov (munching)

Reverence and principles don't feed people.

Pavel

What was it?

Bazarov

Nihilist.

Pavel

Yes. There used to be Hegelians, now there are nihilists. We shall see how you will exist in a void, in a vacuum.

(Arkady returns)

Arkady

We have made friends, Dad! Fedosya Nikolaevna is not quite well today, really. But she will come a little later. But, why didn't you tell me I had a brother?

(Nicolai waves his hand helplessly, Arkady embraces his father)

Nicolai

You must excuse me.

(He exits to the house)

Pavel

Is your special study physics, Mr. Bazarov?

Bazarov

Physics and natural science.

Pavel (ironically)

They say the Teutons have made great progress in that line.

Bazarov

Yes, the Germans are our teachers in it. Their scientists are a clever lot.

Pavel

I dare say you haven't as high an opinion of our Russian scientists.

Bazarov

Very likely—

Pavel

Well, you are not a chauvinist. But if you are a nihilist, surely you don't believe in these Teutons.

Bazarov

They tell me the truth. I agree that's all.

Pavel

Do all Germans tell the truth?

Bazarov (yawning)

Not all.

Pavel

I confess. I don't care for Germans very much. In the past they produced some excellent men, Goethe—Schiller— But now they have all turned chemists and materialists.

Bazarov

A good chemist is twenty times as useful as any poet. An engineer is worth a hundred Goethes.

Pavel

Oh, indeed. You don't acknowledge art, then?

Bazarov (contemptuously)

The art of making money or of advertising pills!

Pavel

Ah—ah— You are pleased to jest, no doubt? Granted. Then, you place your faith in science?

Bazarov

—I have already explained that I don't place my faith anywhere. There are sciences like trades and crafts. But abstract science doesn't exist at all.

Pavel

Very good. And in regard to other accepted traditions of human conduct, do you adopt the same negative attitude?

Bazarov

Is this an examination?

Arkady

Uncle Pavel, please—

Pavel

I am sorry if I have been carried away by the conversation. It's a misfortune to live in the backwoods, as it were, far from mighty intellects. You turn into a fool directly, you try not to forget what you've been taught—but—poof—they'll prove it's all rubbish and that up to date people have no more to do with such foolishness and you are an antiquated old fogy before you're fifty. What's to be done? Young people are, it goes without saying—cleverer than we are.

(Pavel rises, bows and exits into the house)

Bazarov

Is he always like that?

Arkady

I must say, Eugeny, you weren't nice to him. You've hurt his feelings.

Bazarov

I really didn't start it. He should have continued his career if that's his bent. All this vanity and dandyism are a bit out of place a hundred miles from nowhere.

Arkady

He deserves pity rather than ridicule. He's profoundly unhappy. It's a sin to ridicule him.

Bazarov

Who's ridiculing him? He asked my opinion, that's all, and I told him.

(Still eating)

Have some more meat, Arkady, it's delicious. There's no better remedy for idealism than the taste of a good dinner.

Arkady

You're incorrigible.

Bazarov

Of course.

CURTAIN

ACT I
SCENE 2

Nicolai Kirsanov's garden. One or two days later.

Fenitchka is in the garden with a maid, Dunyasha, and her baby. Fenitchka is in the swing, giving the baby a ride. Pavel sees her from the house, hesitates and goes directly to her. Fenitchka jumps out of the swing, in great confusion. She gives the baby to Dunyasha.

Pavel

Stay put. Stay put. Pardon me, if I disturb you—I only wanted to ask you—they are sending into town today, I think—please, let them buy me some green tea.

Fenitchka

Certainly, how much do you want?

Pavel

Oh, half a pound will be enough, I imagine—

(Pause)

I went to your rooms. You have new curtains.

Fenitchka (still embarrassed)

Oh, yes, the curtains. Nicolai Petrovitch was so kind as to make a present of them. They have been up a long time though.

Pavel

It's a long time since I have been to see you. It's very nice now.

Fenitchka

Thanks to Nicolai Petrovitch's kindness.

Pavel

You are more comfortable now, than in the little lodge you used to have?

Fenitchka

Certainly—

Pavel

Who has the lodge now?

Fenitchka

The laundry maids.

Pavel

Ah!

(Pause)

May I see the little one? I love children.

Fenitchka

Dunyasha, please bring Mitya. Ah, he doesn't have a frock on.

Pavel

It doesn't matter. What a chubby fellow.

Fenitchka (to the baby)

That's Uncle.

Pavel

How many months old is he?

Fenitchka

Six months; he will be seven months next week.

Pavel

He's like my brother.

Fenitchka

Who else should he be like?

Pavel

Yes, there's an unmistakable resemblance.

Fenitchka

That's Uncle—

(Nicolai enters from the garden)

Nicolai

Ah, Pavel, so you're here!

Pavel

You've got a splendid little cherub. I came to speak about some tea.

(He bows and returns to the house)

Nicolai

Did he come of himself?

Fenitchka

Yes.

Nicolai

Has Arkady been to see you again?

Fenitchka

No—Hadn't I better move back to the lodge, Nicolai Petrovitch?

Nicolai

Why so?

Fenitchka

I wonder whether it wouldn't be best just for the first?

Nicolai

N-no—we ought to have done it before.

(Turning the baby)

How are you chubby?

(Kisses the baby and then Fenitchka)

Fenitchka

Nicolai Petrovitch, what are you doing?

Nicolai

You're so bashful—

Fenitchka

I can't help it!

Nicolai

It's charming.

(Pause)

So, my brother came to see you?

Fenitchka

Yes.

Nicolai

Well, that's a good thing. I've got to get back to the house. You stay here.

(He exits to the house)

(Bazarov and Arkady enter from the garden)

Bazarov

You ought to have planted silver poplars. Ah, there's someone here.

(Arkady nods to Fenitchka)

Bazarov

Who's that? What a pretty girl!

Arkady

Which one?

Bazarov

Only one of them is pretty.

Arkady

That's Fenitchka, my father's—ah, close friend.

Bazarov

Ah,—your father's got good taste, one can see. I like him, your father. We must make friends, though.

Arkady

Bazarov, mind what you are about.

Bazarov

Don't worry yourself, I know how to behave—I'm not a booby.

(He goes up to Fenitchka, who exhibits great embarrassment, and takes off his cap)

Allow me to introduce myself. I'm a harmless person, and a friend of Arkady Kirsanov.

(Fenitchka rises, too embarrassed to speak)

Bazarov

What a splendid baby! Don't be uneasy— Why is he so red? Is he cutting his teeth?

Fenitchka (strangled)

Yes, four already.

Bazarov

Show me. Don't be afraid, I'm a doctor.

(He examines the baby)

Hmm, hmm. Everything's fine. He'll have a good set of choppers. And you are quite well yourself?

Fenitchka

Yes, thank God.

Bazarov

Thank God, indeed—

(To Dunyasha)

And you?

(Dunyasha giggles)

Well, that's all right. Here's your gallant fellow.

(Returning the baby to Fenitchka)

Fenitchka

How good he was with you!

Bazarov

Children are always good with me.

(He executes quite a gallant bow. Pavel would be surprised if he saw this.)

Well, if anything goes wrong—tell me.

(He returns to Arkady, who has been fidgeting)

Bazarov

What's her name?

Arkady

Fenitchka—Fedosya.

Bazarov

And her father's name?

Arkady

Nikolaevna.

Bazarov

She's all right.

Arkady

She's all right? But my father?

Bazarov

He's all right, too.

Arkady

Well, I don't think so.

Bazarov

You object to the baby?

Arkady

Heavens, no. I think he ought to marry her, that's all.

Bazarov

Well, well, well. You still attach significance to marriage; I didn't expect that of you.

(They walk off)

CURTAIN

ACT I
SCENE 3

Nicolai Kirsanov's garden. The same scene, next day, early morning. A hedge divides the garden so that it is not possible to see over it.

Bazarov is talking to a little boy. He has frogs in a bag.

Boy

What do you want frogs for, Sir?

Bazarov

I'll tell you what for. I shall cut the frog open and see what's going on inside there, and then I shall have a better idea of what's going on inside us.

Boy

Why do you want to know that?

Bazarov

Because I'm a doctor.

Boy

You think I'm the same as a frog? The priest doesn't say that.

Bazarov

Never mind the priest.

Boy

I always mind the priests.

(Arkady comes out of the house)

Arkady

There you are. Up so early.

Bazarov

Frog hunting with my friend here. Run along now.

(The boy leaves)

Arkady

Well, how do you like it?

Bazarov

Well, it's not much to boast of, but quite nice. Quite nice.

Arkady

I hope you like my relations.

Bazarov

Your Uncle is a queer fish. Only fancy, such style in the country. His nails, his nails—you ought to send them to an exhibition.

Arkady

He was a great swell in his day. He used to turn all the women's heads.

Bazarov

Oh, that's it, is it? Keeping up the memory of his conquests. I kept staring at his exquisite collars. They're like marble, and his chin's shaved simply to perfection.

Arkady

But he's a splendid man, really—

Bazarov

An antique survival. But, your father's a capital fellow.

Arkady (warmly)

My father's a man in a thousand.

Bazarov

Did you notice how shy and nervous he is?

Arkady

No.

(Nicolai Petrovitch and Pavel walk by on the other side of the hedge, they stop, overhearing the conversation)

Bazarov

Pity your father spends all his time reading poetry. Forty-four years old and he still reads Pushkin. You ought to tell him.

Arkady

I already have.

Bazarov

Good. Come over this way. I've found a most interesting species of chipmunk.

(Nicolai and Pavel now walk by, talking)

Nicolai

So, it seems you are I are passé—fossils. Well, well, perhaps it's true. I had hoped to get on close terms with Arkady. But he's become a progressive and we can't understand one another.

Pavel

How has he progressed? And in what way is he superior to us? It's that high and mighty gentleman, Sir Nihilist, who's put that into his head. I hate that doctor, I'm convinced he's nothing but an opinionated quack for all his tadpoles!

Nicolai

No, brother, you mustn't say that. He knows his profession.

Pavel

His conceit is revolting.

Nicolai

He is conceited. But, conceit is necessary these days! That's what I didn't take into account. I've tried to keep up. I read all the journals. My neighbors think I'm a Red, and because I lack conceit, my day is over. And I begin to think, maybe it is.

Pavel

Why so?

Nicolai

I'll tell you why. This morning I was sitting, reading Pushkin, when Arkady came up and, without a word, gently took the book from me—just as if I were a baby. In its place he left me this—

Pavel

What is it?

(He examines the book)

Hmm, Arkady is taking your education in hand. Did you try reading it?

Nicolai

Yes, I tried.

Pavel

Well, what did you make of it?

Nicolai

Either I'm stupid, or it's all nonsense!

Pavel

You haven't forgotten your German?

Nicolai

Oh, no—the German is simple enough. I must be stupid, I suppose!

Pavel

Let me have a crack at it.

(He puts it in his pocket)

Nicolai

I just received a letter from Kolyazin.

Pavel

That old windbag?

Nicolai

Himself. He's a bigwig now. He's come to inspect the province and he invites us all to town.

Pavel

Are you going?

Nicolai

I wouldn't dream of it. And you?

Pavel

No. Kolyazin wants to display himself in all his glory. A privy councilor! If I had stayed in the service, I should have done much better than that. Well, he can start without me. Perhaps we could get Bazarov to go. Now, that would be interesting. Besides, I'm behind the times.

Nicolai

Yes, brother, it's time to order a coffin it seems, and make a will.

Pavel

Well, I'm not giving in quite so soon. I've got a tussle with that doctor fellow before me. I'm sure of that.

(Arkady and Bazarov return from viewing the chipmunk)

Pavel

Well, there's Sir Nihilist.

Nicolai

Will you join us for breakfast?

Bazarov (brandishing his bag)

Directly, I have to put these captives away.

Pavel

What have you there, leeches?

Bazarov

No, frogs.

Pavel

Do you eat them, or keep them?

Bazarov

For experiment

(He walks into the house)

Pavel

So, he's going to cut them up. He has no faith in principles, but he has faith in frogs.

Arkady

I do hope you get on better with Bazarov, Uncle. The great thing is, we mustn't pay any attention to him. He doesn't like ceremony.

Pavel

Yes, that's obvious. Is he going to stay with us long?

Arkady

Perhaps. His heart is very good, Uncle.

Pavel

Of course. I wasn't suggesting he was subject to heart attacks.

(he laughs)

CURTAIN

ACT II
SCENE 4

Madame Odinstov's drawing room. A servant shows in Bazarov and Arkady.

Servant

Madame Odinstov will be with you presently.

(He leaves)

Bazarov

Let's see what species of mammalia this specimen belongs to.

(Looks around)

There's something amiss here.

Arkady

What? You, you—Bazarov clinging to narrow morality...?

Bazarov

What a funny fellow you are! Don't you know that something amiss translates to something right in my books? I don't believe the gossip but I like to think its grounded.

Arkady

You're an awful wag at times.

Bazarov

At least I hope she's not too well educated.

Arkady

Why not?

Bazarov

Because in my experience, educated women are the most perfect frights.

Arkady

One would think that you of all people would demand an intellectual woman.

Bazarov

Frankly, I'm interested in their physical attributes.

Arkady

Is it because of her reputation that you wangled this invitation?

Bazarov

Precisely. We need something to divert us if we are to suffer with Uncle Pavel. She has a perfectly scandalous reputation although others say it's undeserved. And she's got the best pair of shoulders I've seen in a long time.

(Looking around)

At any rate she likes to be comfortable, doesn't she? Perhaps we ought to put on evening clothes.

(Enter Anna Sergeyevna Odinstov, widow. She is breathtakingly beautiful in a calm, cool, placid way. She wears an off the shoulder gown. She has, as Bazarov remarked, lovely shoulders. She is perhaps thirty, a couple of years older than Bazarov. Without a doubt she has never truly loved any man. She is followed by her sister who is about seventeen, pretty, but demurely dressed.)

Anna

Thank you for coming. I will not let you go for at least a month. This is Katya, my sister. She plays the piano well—don't you, love?

(Katya curtsies)

And now, let us sit down.

(They all seat themselves. Bazarov is somewhat ill at ease. Anna is having an effect on him that he has never previously experienced. Arkady is dazzled too.)

Is Auntie coming to tea?

Katya

Yes. A little later.

Anna

I should offer you pictures to look at but I can tell you will not like them. Better sit closer and have a conversation.

Bazarov (drawing up his chair)

What subject have you in mind?

Anna

What you like. I warn you, I am dreadfully argumentative.

Bazarov

You!

Anna

Yes. Does that surprise you?

Bazarov

It does.

Anna

Why?

Bazarov

Because you appear to be very cool headed. One must be impulsive to be argumentative.

(Throughout this conversation Katya shows an album to Arkady who feigns interest, but is constantly stealing looks at Anna

Sergeyevna)

Anna

Have you figured me out so quickly? But you are quite wrong. I am impatient and obstinate, ask Katya. And I am very easily carried away.

Bazarov

You know best, I'm sure. But you are wrong to think pictures hold no interest for me.

Anna

Really? I rather suspected you had no artistic feelings.

Bazarov

I haven't. But pictures are frequently more instructive than text in a book. Particularly in anatomy or biology.

Anna

How do you get on without artistic feeling?

Bazarov

What do I need it for?

Anna

Why, to understand men?

Bazarov

Experience enables one to do that. And as individuals go, they're hardly worth it. All people are alike in every basic particular. A botanist wouldn't think of studying individual trees.

Anna

You make it sound so simple. Isn't there a difference between the stupid and the clever, the good and the malevolent?

Bazarov

Only to the extent that these differences can be explained as pathology. We are all made on the same plan. If we are not functioning in the same way, it is due to some external condition. In our case, society. Reform society and you will reform man.

Anna

So, if we reform society, there will be no criminals? No wicked? No insane?

Bazarov

None, except where the defect is organic, as in the case of brain damage.

Anna

And, what is your opinion, Arkady Nicolaievitch?

Arkady

I agree with Eugeny.

Anna

You amaze me, gentlemen. Katya, play something for Arkady Nicolaievitch.

(Katya goes to the piano, followed by Arkady; Katya appears reluctant and Arkady politely indifferent)

Katya

What am I to play for you?

Arkady

What you like. What sort do you like best? Do you like Mozart? Yes?

(Katya begins to play Mozart's Sonata Fantasia in C minor; she plays well, if stiffly)

Anna

We will go for a walk in the garden tomorrow. I want you to teach me the Latin names for the flowers.

Bazarov

Good heavens, why?

Anna

Order is needed in everything.

Arkady (to Katya)

What an exquisite woman your sister is.

Katya (still playing)

Do you think so? Most men do, in fact. Is that enough?

Arkady

It's very lovely.

(He speaks absently, watching Anna and Bazarov who are in an increasingly close tête-à-tête)

Anna (looking up)

I hear Auntie. I expect tea is ready. Will you go in to tea?

(Katya plays some final bars, and escorted by Arkady, follows Anna and Bazarov who continue the tête-à-tête as they exit)

CURTAIN

ACT II
SCENE 5

Anna Sergeyevna's Drawing Room.

Bazarov and Anna Sergeyevna enter, talking.

Bazarov

Everything is so ritualistic here. Liveried servants,—one might as well go to the English style and dine in white tie and tails.

Anna

Perhaps things are a little too formal, but routine is necessary in the country.

Bazarov

Perhaps, but I have the feeling that everything moves "on rails."

Anna

Is that why you are proposing to leave us? What about your promise?

Bazarov

What promise?

Anna

Have you forgotten? You said you would give me some lessons in chemistry.

Bazarov

It can't be helped. My father expects me. However, you can read a book I'll leave you on the subject; it's a good book and clearly written. You will find everything you need in it.

Anna

Why go away?

Bazarov

And, why stay?

Anna

I though perhaps you were enjoying your stay. Perhaps you think you will not be missed here?

Bazarov

I am sure of it.

Anna (quietly)

You are wrong, if you think that. But, I don't believe you mean it. Why don't you be candid?

Bazarov

What am I to say? People are not generally worth being missed and I less than most.

Anna

Why?

Bazarov

I'm a practical, boring person. I don't know how to talk.

Anna

Are you fishing for a compliment, my friend?

Bazarov

That's not a habit of mine. You know very well, I've nothing in common with the elegance you cultivate so well.

Anna

It will be very—boring, without you.

Bazarov

Arkady will remain.

Anna

I will be bored.

Bazarov

Really? In any case, not for long.

Anna

What gives you that idea?

Bazarov

In your well ordered existence, there is no place for boredom—or any disturbing emotions.

Anna

Do you think my life so well ordered?

Bazarov

Without a doubt. As soon as the clock strikes the hour you will drive me away as you usually do at this time.

Anna

No. I won't drive you away. You must stay. Sit down! I want to have a talk with you before you go away. Tell me something about yourself; you never talk about yourself.

Bazarov

I try to talk only on improving subjects.

Anna

You are very modest. But I should like to know something about you. About your family, for whom you are forsaking us.

Bazarov

You are very kind, but we are obscure people.

Anna

You regard me as an aristocrat, a snob!

Bazarov (defiantly)

Yes.

Anna

You know me very little.

Bazarov

That's true. What makes you, with your intellect, with your beauty, invite two obscure students to stay with you?

Anna

What? What was it you said? "With my beauty?"

Bazarov

Never mind that. I meant to say that I don't exactly understand why you have settled in the country.

Anna

How do you explain it yourself?

Bazarov

Why, I assume you do it through a love of comfort, and ease, because you are indifferent to everything else.

Anna

You think me incapable of any great emotion?

Bazarov

Like a kitten. Only curiosity can move you.

Anna

So, you consider me a placid, pampered, spoiled creature?

Bazarov

Undoubtedly.

Anna

Not very chivalrous of you.

Bazarov

I make no pretenses along that line.

Anna

That's why we are such great friends, you are just like me.

Bazarov

Great friends?

(He rises and paces in agitation)

Anna

Where are you going?

(Bazarov by way of reply sinks into a chair)

Anna

You have not discussed how unhappy I am.

Bazarov

You unhappy? What for? Surely you can't attach importance to idle gossip?

Anna

Gossip! Heavens, no. I'm unhappy—miserable is the word, because I am without passion for life. I don't conceal that I like comfort, but I have little desire to live. All romantic nonsense to you!

Bazarov

You are in good health, beautiful, independent, rich. What more do you want?

Anna

What do I want?

Bazarov

Yes?

Anna

Courage.

Bazarov

Are you disillusioned?

Anna

No. Just dissatisfied.

Bazarov

You want to fall in love and you can't love; that's where your unhappiness lies.

Anna

You think I can't fall in love?

Bazarov

You're immune. But I should not call it unhappiness.

Anna

What would you call it?

Bazarov

A misfortune.

Anna

A misfortune? How did you know that?

Bazarov (angrily)

By hearsay.

Anna

My idea is everything or nothing. If you can't have a total commitment, better have nothing.

Bazarov

Those are honorable terms. I'm surprised you haven't found what you wanted.

Anna

It's not easy to find another person like that. Like me.

Bazarov

The chief thing is to be willing to take the leap oneself. Not to worry if someone else will leap with you.

Anna

Isn't that a little reckless?

(Pause)

You speak as though you've experienced all that.

Bazarov

It happened to come up. All that, as you know, is not in my line.

Anna

But, could you take the leap?

Bazarov

I don't know. I don't like to boast.

(He rises)

I'd best be going, it's past your bedtime.

Anna

Wait a little. I want to ask you.

(Pause)

You mentioned a text book?

Bazarov

Yes. It's very good. Fully illustrated and quite up to date. No metaphysical nonsense.

Anna

Eugeny,

(She pauses)

I don't want to talk about that silly book.

Bazarov

In that case....

Anna

I want to speak openly to you.

Bazarov (a little uncomfortable)

As you wish.

Anna

There's no need to tell you, you're well aware yourself, that you are not an ordinary man. What do you want from life? Who are you? What are you?

Bazarov

You surprise me. You know I am studying natural science and—

Anna (earnestly)

Who are you?

Bazarov

I am going to be a district doctor.

Anna

What do you say that for? You don't believe it yourself. Arkady might answer me that way, but not you.

Bazarov

In what way is Arkady—

Anna

Stop. Is it possible that you could content yourself with such a humble career? You with your ambition? A district doctor? Don't put me off like you would a child or a stranger.

Bazarov

I am not in the habit of talking about my ambitions freely, and between us there is such a gulf.

Anna

What sort of gulf? Are you telling me I'm an aristocratic snob again?

Bazarov

The future does not depend on us. If a chance turns up to do something, so much the better. If not, better not have gossiped about it.

Anna

Is this kind of explanation idle gossip? Or do you consider me, as a woman, unworthy of your confidence? I know you have a low opinion of women.

Bazarov

I don't despise you, Anna Sergeyevna! And you know that!

Anna

I don't know anything! I can understand your unwillingness to talk about your dreams of the future, but I don't see why you can't speak freely of what is in your heart.

Bazarov

Can you?

Anna (firmly)

Yes.

Bazarov (bowing)

You are more fortunate than I am.

Anna

As you please. But, I am sure this constraint, this reticence will vanish at last.

Bazarov

So you have noticed reticence, constraint, as you put it?

Anna

Yes.

Bazarov

And would you like to know the reason for this reticence? Would you like to know what is passing within me?

Anna (a bit frightened)

Yes.

Bazarov

And you will not be angry?

Anna

No.

Bazarov

No? Then, let me tell you that I love you like a fool, like a madman! There you have forced it out of me!

Anna (tenderly)

Eugeny

(Bazarov embraces her ferociously, not like a timed child but like a passionate man)

Bazarov

Well, are you insulted?

Anna

No.

Bazarov

Well?

Anna (whispering)

You have misunderstood me.

Bazarov

Am I to go today?

Anna (arranging herself)

Why should you go? I did not understand you—you did not understand me.

(Slightly awkward)

I did not understand myself, either. I am to blame—

Bazarov

I have to apologize to you, Anna Sergeyevna. You must be in a fury with me.

Anna

No. I'm not angry with you, but I am sorry.

Bazarov

So much the worse, Anyway, I am sufficiently punished. My position, you will certainly agree, is most foolish. Tomorrow I shall be gone.

Anna

I am to blame. I did not foresee this. Eugeny, I would rather you stayed.

Bazarov

There's no recalling the past, Anna. And this was bound to

come about sooner or later.

(Pause)

So, I must go.

(Pause)

Excuse my impertinence, but you don't love me and you never will love me, I suppose?

(Anna does not answer, but although Bazarov takes it her answer is "no", there is evidence that the reason for her silence is that the answer is "yes")

Anna

I am to blame.

Bazarov

Goodbye then.

Anna

We shall meet again shan't we? Before you go?

Bazarov

As you command.

Anna

In that case, we shall.

(Bazarov leaves, a short pause, Katya enters)

Katya

Is it all right?

Anna

No. It's not all right. I wanted him to declare himself and he has.

Katya

Well, then?

Anna

I'm afraid of him.

Katya

You, afraid of a man?

(Anna laughs throatily)

Anna

Yes, me! At last. God knows what it will lead to. He can't be played with.

(Pause)

Anyway, peace is the best thing.

Katya

I think you love him.

CURTAIN

ACT III
SCENE 6

Bazarov's family home. The Bazarov home is cramped and confined. We are in the living room. It is hung with pictures, icons, knick-knacks. Old Bazarov is a benign, bearded old man of about sixty. He is pacing up and down, dressed in a military coat which he wears unbuttoned. The room, like its master, is shabby genteel, but there is no constraint about it. Such as it is, it is a happy home. A door at the left leads to the porch; another on the right leads to the living quarters.

Suddenly, Old Bazarov rushes out and we hear his voice.

Old Bazarov

Arrived, at last! Come, get out; get out; let me hug you.

(Bazarov, Old Bazarov and Arkady enter from the door at the audience's left)

Old Bazarov

Finally, you see everything is just the same.

(Bazarov is bearing this effusion of emotion with as much grace as he can, which isn't much, because he knows he is in for more)

(Madame Bazarov watched from the door at the right, crying "Enyusha, my baby, my baby." She is a plump, little, old woman in a white cap and a striped jacket. She is almost fainting with emotion. She embraces Bazarov who winks at Arkady with a long suffering expression.)

Old Bazarov

That's enough, that's enough, old woman—give over.

(Madame Bazarov continues to hang on her son's neck, making the following fulsome excuse)

Madame Bazarov

For what ages! Now, I have my dear one, my darling, again.

Old Bazarov

Well, to be sure, it's in the nature of things. Women are weak. A mother's heart.

Bazarov

Let us come in, Mother. We'd really like to sit.

(Bazarov is, on the whole, surprisingly gentle with his parents)

This is Arkady Nicolaievitch.

Old Bazarov

Heartily glad to make your acquaintance. But you mustn't expect great things.

(To his wife)

Mother, calm yourself, please. This gentleman, our guest, will think ill of you.

Madame Bazarov

My dear sir, I am so pleased.

Arkady

And, I, too.

Madame Bazarov

You must excuse a silly old woman like me. You see, I thought I wouldn't live to see my dar-ling—

(She cries again)

Old Bazarov

Well, you see, we have lived to see him, as I promised you, many times.

(He calls a servant, a small ragged girl)

Bring your mistress a glass of water and these gentlemen vodka.

(Pause)

On a tray, mind you.

Madame Bazarov (as the servant exits)

Let me embrace you just once more. Why, how handsome you have grown!

Old Bazarov

Well, I don't know about being handsome, but he is a real man. Now, I hope, old woman, that having satisfied your mother's heart, you will turn your thoughts to satisfying the appetites of our guests.

Madame Bazarov (rising from her chair)

This minute! I will run myself to the kitchen. Everything shall be ready, everything.

(She hurries out)

Old Bazarov

Don't put us to shame, good woman.

(To Arkady)

I warn you, my dear, Arkady Nicolaievitch, we live rather rough here.

Bazarov (interrupting, irritated, but not unkind)

Stop that, what are you apologizing for? My friend knows we are not rich. The question is, where are we to put him?

Old Bazarov

In the little lodge, perhaps?

Bazarov

That sounds good.

Old Bazarov

I will run over there at once.

(He runs out, left)

Bazarov

There you have him! Comical old fellow, but very good natured. He chatters too much.

Arkady

Your mother seems awfully nice.

Bazarov

Wait till you see the dinner she'll give us.

Arkady

How many serfs has your father?

Bazarov

Fifteen, in all. Of course, they're free now.

(Pause)

Well, brother, we are here. So, in spite of all the discomforts of life, man must go and invent others for himself.

Arkady

What are you alluding to?

Bazarov

Alluding? I'm saying it straight out. We've both behaved like fools. What's the use of talking about it! Still, a man who's furious to be ill, invariably gets well.

Arkady

I should have thought you have nothing to complain of.

Bazarov

Don't you? I'll say this, it's better to be a slave than to let a woman have power over the tip of your little finger. It's all rubbish. A man hasn't time to attend to such trifles. As the Spanish say, "a man ought not to be tame!"

Arkady

I'm surprised she let you go.

Bazarov

I'm not her servant, after all.

Arkady

Ah, is that why you're so melancholy?

Bazarov

You'll get old if you know too much.

Arkady

I'm rather sorry to lose Katya.

Bazarov

We have taken a beating, Arkady. That's what comes of being educated people.

(Arkady gives a forced laugh. There is an uncomfortable pause. Old Bazarov returns, jubilant.)

Old Bazarov (to Arkady)

In a few minutes your room will be ready to receive you. You smoke, sir?

(Offering a pipe)

Arkady

I generally smoke cigars.

Old Bazarov

You do very sensibly. I, myself, prefer them, but unfortunately in these wilds, they are rather hard to come by.

Bazarov

That's enough humble pie. You'd do much better to sit here on the sofa and let us have a look at you.

(Old Bazarov laughs and sits. He is very like his son in build and feature, but whereas his son's predominating trait is gruffness, his is affability and politeness bordering on unctuousness. It is quite probable that the younger Bazarov's manners were adopted in rebellion against his father's excessive optimism, cordiality and impracticality.)

(The servant returns and serves tea, then exits)

Old Bazarov

Humble pie! You mustn't assume I wish to appeal to our guest's sympathies. Quite the contrary.

Bazarov

I see you have here "The Friend of Health for 1855."

Old Bazarov (proudly)

It was sent me by an old comrade out of friendship. We are not completely out of date We even have some small idea of phrenology.

Bazarov

Do people still believe in phrenology in these parts?

Old Bazarov (coughing)

In these parts, of course, you know best. How could we keep pace with you? In my day there was a sort of humorist theory, all very ridiculous to us, although it had once dominated medical thinking. Something new has taken the place of phrenology. You bow down to it. But in twenty years, that, too, will be replaced.

Bazarov

If it's any consolation to you we laugh at medicine. We don't bow down to anything.

Old Bazarov

But you're going to be a doctor? Aren't you?

Bazarov

All the more reason.

Old Bazarov

Well, perhaps. What do I know? I was merely an army surgeon.

Arkady

You were in my grandfather's brigade.

Old Bazarov

Yes, yes. Your grandfather was a very honorable man. A real soldier.

Bazarov

Confess, he was rather a blockhead.

Old Bazarov

How can you say such a thing? General Kirsanov?

Bazarov

Come, drop him. Let's change the subject.

(Changing the subject)

Driving in, I was pleased to see that birch copse has shot up.

Old Bazarov

You must see what a little garden I've got now! All kinds of fruit and medicinal herbs. I've retired from active practice, you know. But two or three times a week, a peasant will come for help. I can't very well drive them away. And there are no doctors here at all.

Arkady

No doctors at all? How uncivilized.

Old Bazarov

Yes, yes, of course. We do what we can.

(Old Bazarov notices his wife advancing from the kitchen)

You must be magnanimous and pardon me if I've bored you. I dare say my good wife will give more satisfaction.

Madame Bazarov

Dinner is ready!

(Madame Bazarov is in a state of elation. She has put on a cap with ribbons and a pale blue flowered shawl. Directly she looks at Bazarov, however, her composure breaks. She quickly wipes away a tear.)

Bazarov

Come, Arkady. I will show you the way. One thing's a bother. My mother's so tender hearted, if you don't grow round as a tub and eat ten times a day she gets all fussed.

(Bazarov leads Arkady off at the door to the right)

Madame Bazarov (to her husband)

My—ba-by!

(She bawls)

Old Bazarov

There, there now, old woman. How long does he intend to stay? I don't dare ask him myself.

(Bawling)

What if he only stays for two days?

SHORT CURTAIN

ACT III
SCENE 7

Bazarov's garden. Several garden chairs.

Old Bazarov is seated, reading, when Arkady enters.

Old Bazarov

The best of health to you. How have you slept?

Arkady

Capitally.

Old Bazarov

Here I am, you see, reading. Half an hour ago, you should have seen me in a totally different position laying out a bed for turnips. You, I know, are accustomed to luxury, but even the great ones of this world do not disdain to spend a brief time under a cottage roof.

Arkady

As if I were a great one or accustomed to luxury!

Old Bazarov

Pardon me, pardon me. I can tell a bird by its flight. I tell you, without flattery, I am sincerely delighted at the friendship I observe between you and my son. Permit me to inquire! Have you known him long?

Arkady

Since last winter.

Old Bazarov

Indeed. Permit me to ask you, as a father, without reserve, please. What do you think of my son?

Arkady (sincerely)

Your son is the most remarkable man I have ever met.

Old Bazarov (agitated)

You really mean that?

Arkady

I'm convinced that your son has a great future ahead of him and that he will do great honor to your name.

Old Bazarov (beaming)

You have made me perfectly happy. I should tell you that I idolize my son; I won't speak of my wife, everyone knows how mothers are! But, I don't dare show my feelings before him; he doesn't like it. He hates any show of feeling, many people find fault with him for that. But, it's not for want of feeling, just firmness of character. Would you believe it, from the day he was born, he would never accept a penny more than he could help from me? That's God's truth!

Arkady

He is a disinterested, honest man.

Old Bazarov

Exactly so. And one day I hope in his biography...I am sure he will have a biography, it will say "The son of a simple army doctor who spared nothing for his education."

Arkady (presses his hand)

You are very good. I know he loves you.

Old Bazarov

Do you think it will be in medicine that he will attain distinction?

Arkady

No. Although he will be one of its leading lights.

Old Bazarov

In what then?

Arkady

Who knows? But, rest assured, he will be famous.

Old Bazarov

He will be famous!

(A servant enters from the house)

Servant

Your wife sent me to call you in to tea.

Old Bazarov

Serve it here.

Servant

Yes, Sir.

(Returns to the house)

Old Bazarov

Why is it my son hasn't come?

Bazarov (entering from the garden)

I'm here.

Old Bazarov

Aha. You are too late, my friend. I have already had a long conversation with your colleague. By the way, I want to consult with you.

Bazarov

About what?

Old Bazarov

There's a peasant here suffering from icterus.

Bazarov

You mean jaundice?

Old Bazarov

Yes, I've prescribed for him, but it isn't helping much. Though you laugh at medicine, I'm certain you can give me practical advice. Ah—here's tea.

(The servant enters with a samovar and serves tea to all. As tea is being served, another servant enters.)

Second Servant

Major Bazarov, you are needed. There is a peasant to see you about a sick horse.

Old Bazarov

Such are the duties of country life. Please excuse me, gentlemen.

(He goes off into the house humming a lovely tune)

Bazarov

Singular vitality.

(He laughs)

Arkady

Has this house been standing long?

Bazarov

Yes, my grandfather built it.

Arkady

Who was he? Your grandfather?

Bazarov

Devil knows. He served with Suvarov.

Arkady

Yes, I've seen the portrait of Suvarov in the drawing room. I like these dear little old houses like yours. They're so cozy.

Bazarov (unsentimentally)

Unfortunately, they're full of flies. Faugh!

(Pause)

Arkady

Tell me, were they strict with you when you were a child?

Bazarov

Those two cream puffs? You can imagine what they were like.

I've run them since I was five or so.

Arkady

Are you fond of them?

Bazarov

I am, Arkady.

Arkady

They are fond of you, too.

(Pause)

Bazarov

Do you know what I am thinking?

Arkady

No?

Bazarov

I'm thinking my parents are very happy. My father is still fussing around doctoring people, playing bountiful master with the peasants, and mother is bustling about the house; while I....

Arkady

While you?

Bazarov

While I think and brood. Isn't it loathsome?

Arkady

Isn't everybody that way?

Bazarov

Yes, when we're young. I feel nothing but weariness and anger.

Arkady

Anger? Why anger?

Bazarov

Have you forgotten?

Arkady

You're unlucky in love, but I don't see any reason for anger.

Bazarov

You are one of those men who cluck, cluck, to the hen, but if the hen approaches, you run. I'm not like that.

(Pause)

Enough of this. It can't be helped and it's degrading to talk about it. Look, see that ant dragging away a fly.

(To the ant)

Take her, brother, take her. It's your privilege to be free of pity, make the most of it, not like us conscience-stricken self-destructive animals.

Arkady

But you haven't destroyed yourself.

Bazarov

Amen. And no woman is going to crush me. You won't hear another word from me about it.

Arkady

You're in a melancholy mood today.

Bazarov

It's pettiness, pettiness that's insufferable.

Arkady

Pettiness doesn't exist if you refuse to recognize.

Bazarov

That's an idea! A real man ought not to care. Unfortunately, it's hard to stifle the hate.

(Pause)

Arkady

It's funny. I don't hate anybody.

Bazarov

That's because you don't have a very high opinion of yourself. I hate so many.

Arkady

You have a high opinion of yourself, then?

Bazarov

That's obvious, isn't it? And the more I see of people, the more my opinion grows. Most people are scum, Arkady. Particularly our beloved peasantry, for whom I'm supposed to sacrifice myself when the revolution comes. They won't even thank us for it. And what do we gain by it? Our love of humanity! Pah!

Arkady

Isn't it a matter of principle?

Bazarov (viciously)

You talk like your Uncle. There are no principles.

Arkady

What a depressing thought.

Bazarov

Not to your taste, brother? Well, once you've made up your mind to mow down everything, don't spare your own legs. I like to deny, to negate, my brain's made on that plan. That's all there is to it. Deeper than that, man will never penetrate and frankly he's a fool to try.

Arkady

But, surely man is better than that. For example—

Bazarov (savagely)

No fine talk, Arkady. No fine talk.

Arkady

I talk the best I can. You're being despotic. I have an idea, why shouldn't I express it?

Bazarov

Just so. And why shouldn't I express my ideas? Fine talk is positively indecent.

Arkady

And is rudeness decent?

Bazarov

You really do intend to walk in your Uncle's footsteps. How pleased that worthy imbecile would have been if he could hear you.

Arkady (hotly)

What did you call my Uncle?

Bazarov (coolly)

I called him an imbecile. Aha! Family feeling spoke there. How obstinately it speaks in people!

Arkady (indignantly)

It was a simple sense of justice and not the least family feeling. But since you don't have such ideas, you can't appreciate them in others.

Bazarov (mockingly)

In other words, Arkady Kirsanov is too exalted for my comprehension.

(Bowing)

I must acknowledge your superiority and say no more.

Arkady

Eugeny, stop. We shall end by quarreling!

Bazarov

Ah, Arkady, do me a favor, let's quarrel for once in earnest.

Arkady

But, we shall end by—

Bazarov

Fighting? What does it mater? But you're no match for me. I'd have you by the throat, like that!

(He gestures)

In a minute!

Old Bazarov (returning)

Ah, you're still here?

Bazarov (in an undertone)

Pity he interrupted us.

Old Bazarov

When I look at you, my youthful friends, I cannot refrain from admiration. You are like the Dioscuri, a veritable Castor and Pollux.

Bazarov

Come, shut up, father. Don't show off your Latin.

Old Bazarov

Once in a while it's surely permissible. However, I am not here to pay you compliments, but with the object, first, of announcing that the village priest will be dining with us.

Bazarov

Father Alexey?

Old Bazarov

Well, yes, he is to dine with us. I did not anticipate this, and do not even approve it, but somehow it came about.

Bazarov

He won't eat my dinner, will he?

Old Bazarov

How you talk!

Bazarov (his good humor returning)

Well, that's all I ask. I'm ready to sit down to table with any man.

Old Bazarov

I was certain before I spoke that you were above any kind of prejudice. You will like him. You see, your mother wished to have a Te Deum sung on the occasion of your arrival.

Bazarov

What?

Old Bazarov (placatingly)

Oh, it's all over now. And Father Alexey wished to make your acquaintance. You will see. He even plays whist.

Bazarov

Good, I'll clean him out.

Old Bazarov

That remains to be seen. You play too rashly.

Bazarov

Napoleon's rule, father. Napoleon's rule.

Old Bazarov

You see where it got him.

(He goes back into the house)

I must tell your mother.

Bazarov

I'll bet he did it himself.

Arkady

What?

Bazarov

Ordered that *Te Deum*.

Arkady

You think so?

Bazarov

He's just as religious as she is. Well, that's it. I'm off from here tomorrow. I want to work and I can't work here. I'll go back to your father's, if you'll let me.

Arkady

Of course.

Bazarov

I'm sorry I got that way. I don't usually apologize for anything, but I want to apologize for that.

Arkady

It's all right, brother.

Bazarov

Good.

(Pause)

In your house I can shut myself up. Here, my father says "My study is at your disposal" and he hovers around like a mother hen. And I can hear mother sighing on the other side of the wall. And if you try talking, there's nothing to say.

Arkady

She will be very much grieved.

Bazarov

I'll come again. Life is not over.

Arkady

I feel sorry for your mother.

Bazarov

Has she won your heart with strawberries?

Arkady

She's very clever really. We talked for half an hour yesterday.

Bazarov

About me, I suppose?

Arkady

Not at all.

Bazarov

Well, if a woman can talk sensibly for a half hour, it's a hopeful sign. But, I'm going all the same.

Arkady

It won't be easy to break it to them.

Bazarov

No, it won't be easy. I shall have to upset them more than ever. Never mind. Never say die! He'll get over it.

(Old Bazarov returns)

Old Bazarov

Well, well, everything's all arranged.

Bazarov (to Arkady)

Well, it's now or never.

(To Old Bazarov)

Oh, I almost forgot to tell you. We'll need the horses tomorrow.

Old Bazarov

Is Arkady leaving us then?

Bazarov

Yes, and I'm going with him.

Old Bazarov (staggered)

You are going?

Bazarov

Yes, I must.

Old Bazarov

Very good, of course, only— How is it?

Bazarov

I must stay with him a little time. I will return later.

Old Bazarov

Ah, for a little time. Very good. Well, everything will be taken care of. I had hoped you were to be with us a little longer. Three days, after three years, it is rather little. Rather little.

Bazarov

But, I'm coming back in a few weeks. It's necessary for me to go.

Old Bazarov

Well, duty first, I suppose. Very good. Your mother and I, of course, did not anticipate this. She had just decided to redecorate your room.

Bazarov

It will be ready when I return then.

Old Bazarov

Freedom is the best thing. I do not wish to hamper you.

Bazarov

We shall soon see each other again, father, really.

Old Bazarov

Of course. Of course.

Bazarov

What do you say to a walk, Arkady?

Arkady

Sounds good.

(They go into the garden)

(Madame Bazarov enters)

Madame Bazarov

What is the matter, dear?

Old Bazarov

Nothing, never mind. Don't worry yourself.

Madame Bazarov

Is Enyusha all right?

Old Bazarov

He's all right.

Madame Bazarov

Do you know I'm afraid he might not be comfortable on that bed? I should have given him our feather bed but he doesn't like too soft a bed.

Old Bazarov

He is going, mother.

Madame Bazarov

What?

Old Bazarov

He has cast us off. He has forsaken us. He is dull with us. Lord, have mercy on me for a poor sinner.

Madame Bazarov (proving the stronger of the two)

There's no help for it, my dear. Don't grieve. A son is like a falcon. He must fly off at his pleasure. You and I are like twigs in a nest, and don't move from our place. Only I am left you, as you for me. We must wait. And pray God.

(They embrace)

CURTAIN

ACT IV
SCENE 8

The garden of Nicolai Petrovitch Kirsanov.

Nicolai Petrovitch, Pavel, Arkady, and Bazarov are seated, having tea.

Nicolai

Well, did you enjoy your stay with Madame Odinstov?

Bazarov

We came to look at the gentry and we had a look at them.

Pavel

She is a great aristocrat.

(Without realizing how badly he is treading on Bazarov's toes)

Bazarov

She is a rotten, aristocratic snob.

Pavel

Allow me to ask you, according to your ideas, have the words "rotten" and "aristocratic" the same meaning?

Bazarov (drinking his tea)

I said rotten, aristocratic snob.

Pavel

Precisely so. But, I suspect you have the same opinions of aristocrats as of aristocratic snobs.

Bazarov

And, if I do?

Pavel

I think it my duty to inform you that I do not share your opinion; that's all.

Bazarov

Well, that was to be expected before either of us opened his mouth.

Pavel

Everyone knows me for a man of liberal views. I am not a reactionary. But, for that very reason, I respect aristocrats, real aristocrats.

Bazarov

Very good

Pavel

Kindly remember, Sir. Kindly remember, Sir, the English aristocracy. They do not abate one iota of their rights and for that reason they respect the rights of others. The aristocracy has given freedom to England.

Bazarov

We have heard that story, many times. What are you trying to prove by it?

Pavel

I am trying to prove by that, Sir, that without a sense of personal dignity, without self-respect there is no cure foundation for the social order.

Bazarov

Assuming I admit that, what then?

Pavel

Personal character is the chief thing. It is the rock society is built on. I am well aware that you are pleased to consider my dress, my habits, my refinements,—ridiculous. But, all that proceeds from a sense of self-respect. Indeed, from a sense of duty. I live in the wild, but I will now lower myself.

Bazarov (rising and folding his arms)

Let me ask you, Pavel Petrovitch. You respect yourself and sit with your hands folded; what sort of benefit does that confer on society? If you didn't respect yourself, you would still do nothing.

Pavel (mortally insulted)

That's a different question. I do not have to explain to you why I sit with my hands folded as you are pleased to express it. I am talking about principles. Only immoral and silly people can live without principles. I said so to Arkady right after he came home. Didn't I, Nicolai?

(Nicolai nods)

Bazarov

Aristocracy, liberalism, progress, principles,—foreign words, and useless to a Russian.

Pavel

What is good for something according to you? If we listen to you, we shall find ourselves outside humanity, outside its laws.

Bazarov

We can get on without that, too. You don't need laws to put bread in your mouth when you're hungry. What's the use of these abstractions to us?

Pavel

I don't understand you! How is it possible to act if you don't acknowledge principles?

Arkady

I've told you already, Uncle, that we don't accept any authorities.

Bazarov

We act by virtue of what we recognize as beneficial. At the present time negation is beneficial.

Pavel

And, you deny everything?

Bazarov

Everything.

Nicolai

But, one must construct, too, you know.

Bazarov

That's not our business, now. The ground wants clearing first.

Arkady

The present condition of the people requires it.

Pavel (energetically)

No! No! I'm not willing to believe that you know the Russian people. It is a patriarchal people; it cannot live without faith and tradition.

Bazarov

I'm not going to dispute that. I'm even willing to agree you are right.

Pavel

But, if I am right, it proves nothing?

Arkady

Nothing at all.

Pavel

How does it prove nothing? You must be going against the people then?

Bazarov

What if we are? The peasants believe the earth rests on three fishes. Are we to agree with them? But am I not a Russian, too?

Pavel

No. You are not a Russian.

Bazarov

My grandfather ploughed the land. Ask any of your peasants which of us he would acknowledge as a Russian. Besides, you don't even know how to talk to them.

Pavel

Perhaps not, but I don't despise them either.

Bazarov

Suppose they deserve contempt? My attitude is a product of the same national spirit you have just been defending.

Pavel

So, that's it. Nihilism is to cure all our woes, and you, you are our heroes and saviors.

Arkady

Yes, we've had enough of perpetual talk.

Pavel

Don't you talk as much as everyone else?

Bazarov

Whatever faults we have, we do not err in that way.

Pavel

Well, then? Do you act, or what? Are you preparing for action?

Bazarov

Why, even you suppose you're not a useless person.

Nicolai

Gentlemen, gentlemen, no personalities, please.

Pavel

Don't be uneasy. I shall not forget myself. H'mmm, action, destruction, but how destroy without even knowing? Why?

Bazarov

We shall destroy because we are a force.

Arkady

A force is not accountable.

Pavel

Unhappy boy! If you could only realize what you are doing to our country. Force. There's force in the Tatars, but what is that to us? What is precious to us is civilization. And, don't tell me civilization is worthless. The humblest shoemaker represents civilization. You fancy yourselves advanced people and yet you worship power like a savage. Recollect the people are millions who will crush you rather than permit you to destroy their sacred traditions.

Bazarov

If we're crushed it serves us right. But only time will tell. And, don't think we're so few as you suppose. All Moscow was burnt down by one man.

Pavel

Yes, yes. First, a pride almost Satanic, then ridicule, that's what gains ascendancy over inexperienced youth. There's one of them sitting beside you, ready to worship the ground under your feet. Look at him.

(Arkady turns away)

In the old days men had to study. Now they need only say everything is silly and the trick's done. To be sure, they were simply geese before, and now they have suddenly turned nihilists.

Bazarov

Your praiseworthy sense of personal dignity has given way. Our argument has gone too far. Better to cut it short, I think. I shall be quite ready to agree with you when you bring forward a single institution worthy of preservation.

Pavel

I will bring forward not one, but millions.

Bazarov

Think it over, carefully. Meanwhile Arkady and I—

Pavel

Will continue to ridicule everything.

Bazarov

No, we'll go on dissecting frogs. Come, Arkady. Goodbye, for the present, gentlemen.

(They go off into the garden)

Pavel

So that's what they are like—our successors.

Nicolai

Our successors! I remember telling mother once that she couldn't understand me because we belonged to two different generations. She was dreadfully offended. You see. Now our turn has come.

Pavel

You are beyond everything in generosity and modesty. I'm convinced that you and I are more nearly right than they, though we are forced to express ourselves in an old fashioned way, and have not the same insolent conceit and swagger of these young people.

Nicolai

Do you know? Bazarov it seems to me is more of an aristocrat than any of us.

Pavel (stupefied)

Bazarov, how?

Nicolai

He is proud, he doesn't give a damn for anyone's opinion of him. He is totally uncompromising, courageous—

Pavel

But refinement, breeding, manners?

Nicolai

Those he regards as superfluous.

Pavel

But, are they?

Nicolai

I hope not. I hope not.

Fenitchka (popping in from the house)

Would anyone like more tea?

Nicolai

No, tell them to take the samovar. I've had all the tea I can stomach!

(Nicolai, Pavel, and Fenitchka retire into the house. After a brief pause, Bazarov and Arkady enter.)

Arkady

I think you really hurt Uncle Pavel's feelings.

Bazarov

Is he always like that?

Arkady

You weren't nice to him.

Bazarov

Enough of him. He should have continued his career in Petersburg if that's his bent. I've found a rare species of water beetle. Dytiscus morginatus, do you know it?

Arkady

I promised to tell you his story.

Bazarov

The story of the beetle?

Arkady

The story of my Uncle! He deserves pity rather than ridicule.

Bazarov

How so?

Arkady

You see, he fell in love with a Princess. She was married and had many lovers. First, he succeeded, then she grew cold toward him. Then she died. He suffered greatly. In short, it's a sin to despise him.

Bazarov

A man who stakes his whole life on a woman is fit for nothing, he's not a man.

Arkady

But remember, his education.

Bazarov

Education? Every man must educate himself! It's all nonsense. He had much better dissect this beetle.

(They exit as the **CURTAIN FALLS**)

ACT IV
SCENE 9

Several weeks later in Nicolai Kirsanov's garden.

Fenitchka is sitting on a garden seat. In her lap a whole heap of red and white roses.

Bazarov enters.

Fenitchka

Oh, Mr. Bazarov, what are you doing here?

Bazarov

Making a nosegay?

Fenitchka

Yes, for the table at lunch. Nicolai Petrovitch likes it.

Bazarov

It's a long time yet to lunch. What a heap of flowers!

Fenitchka

I went out early because it will be too hot later. I feel a little weak even now.

Bazarov

Let me feel your pulse.

(He takes it)

You'll live a hundred years.

Fenitchka

God forbid.

Bazarov

Oh, you want to be young?

Fenitchka

Yes, it is better.

Bazarov

How so?

Fenitchka

Why, because I can do everything.

Bazarov

Age makes no difference to me.

Fenitchka

I don't believe you.

Bazarov

Judge for yourself. I live alone.

Fenitchka

But that depends on you.

Bazarov

Not at all. Someone must take pity on me to change that.

Fenitchka

What's that book you have?

Bazarov

That? Oh, Karl Marx.

Fenitchka

Are you still studying?

Bazarov

Yes. You should try to read a little.

Fenitchka

Oh—I don't understand anything. What a thick book.

(She tries to read, it is obvious that she is barely literate)

Bazarov

You're pretty when you read. The end of your nose moves so nicely.

(Fenitchka laughs)

I like it when you laugh.

Fenitchka

Nonsense.

Bazarov

And when you talk, too.

Fenitchka

Pshah, you've talked with such clever ladies.

Bazarov

Believe me all the clever ladies in the world are not worth your little finger.

Fenitchka

What a tease you are. But I want to thank you for that medicine you prescribed for Mitya. He sleeps like a lamb now.

Bazarov

But you have to pay doctors. Doctors you know are grasping

people.

Fenitchka

I'd be delighted. But, I must ask Nicolai Petrovitch.

Bazarov

Do you think I want money? No, I don't want money.

Fenitchka

What, then?

Bazarov

Guess.

Fenitchka

How am I to know?

Bazarov

Well, I will tell you. One of those roses.

Fenitchka

By all means. A red or white?

Bazarov

Red, and not too large.

Fenitchka

Here, take it.

Bazarov

What's wrong?

Fenitchka

I thought someone was coming.

Bazarov

Nicolai Petrovitch?

Fenitchka

No. Besides, I'm not afraid of him. I thought it was Pavel Petrovitch.

Bazarov

Why are you afraid of him?

Fenitchka

He always scares me. And I know you don't like each other. You always spin him around.

Bazarov

Suppose he drubbed me. Would you stand up for me?

Fenitchka

Me? But, no one can get the better of you.

Bazarov

It's nice of you to say so. This rose smells delicious. I'd like you to smell it with me.

(She leans over to smell it and Bazarov kisses her. She protests somewhat feebly. There is a cough. Fenitchka jumps up and runs off)

Fenitchka

It was wrong of you.

(Pavel enters)

Pavel (dryly)

I must apologize for hindering your scientific pursuits, but I must beg you to spare me five minutes of your time.

Bazarov

You may have as long as you like.

Pavel

Five minutes will be enough for me. I want to put a single question to you.

Bazarov

A question? What about?

Pavel

At the commencement of your stay, before I renounced the pleasure of conversing with you, I heard your opinion on many subjects, but so far as my memory serves, you never expressed yourself on dueling. Allow me to hear your views on that subject.

Bazarov (folding his arms)

Theoretically, it's silly, but from a practical standpoint, quite another matter.

Pavel

If I understand you, regardless of your views, you would not allow yourself to be insulted?

Bazarov

Exactly.

Pavel

You relieve my mind. You see I have made up my mind to fight you.

Bazarov

Me?

Pavel

Undoubtedly.

Bazarov

But, what for?

Pavel

I prefer not to explain. To my mind, your presence here is superfluous. I cannot endure you, I despise you. Is that enough?

Bazarov

Perfectly. I see no need for further explanations.

Pavel

I am sensible of my obligation to you, and may reckon then on your accepting my challenge without compelling me to resort to violent measures?

Bazarov

You mean that stick? It is unnecessary and perhaps not a perfectly safe proceeding. I accept your challenge.

Pavel

Excellent. I should like to know whether you think it necessary to resort to the pretext of a trifling quarrel.

Bazarov

No, there's no need for that.

Pavel

For once, we are in agreement. We cannot endure one another.

Bazarov

What more is necessary?

Pavel

As regards seconds, there will be none, for where could be get them?

Bazarov

Agreed.

Pavel

Then I have the honor to suggest that the combat take place tomorrow at dawn, over there in the fields, at ten paces.

Bazarov

That will do. We hate the sight of each other at that distance.

Pavel

We might make it at eight. Let us each put a suicide note in his pocket.

Bazarov

Now, that I don't approve of. It has the unsavory flavor of a French novel.

Pavel

Perhaps. But you will agree it would be unpleasant to incur a suspicion of murder?

Bazarov

True. But, there's a better way. We can have a witness.

Pavel

Allow me to inquire, whom?

Bazarov

Why, Piotr.

Pavel

I think you are joking, Sir.

Bazarov

Not at all. I shall manage it.

Pavel

You persist in jesting, still. But after the courteous readiness you have shown me, I cannot complain. And so, everything is arranged. By the way, do you have pistols?

Bazarov

How should I, dear Sir? I am a student, not in the army.

Pavel

In that case, I offer you mine. You may rest assured, I have not fired them in five years.

Bazarov

That's very consoling news.

Pavel

And now, my dear, Sir, it only remains for me to thank you and to leave you to your studies.

Bazarov (bowing)

Till we have the pleasure of meeting, again, my dear, Sir.

(Pavel goes toward the house.)

I'll bet he's after her himself. And just when I had finally assumed the role of Gay Lothario.

(Arkady enters)

Arkady

Ah, there you are, Bazarov.

Bazarov

I am here.

Arkady

I've decided to pay a visit to Anna Sergeyevna. Would you like to come?

Bazarov

When are you leaving?

Arkady

In the morning.

Bazarov

No. I have some unfinished work to attend to. Besides, I'm not welcome there any more.

CURTAIN

ACT IV
SCENE 10

A field, trees in the background.

Piotr and Bazarov are waiting for Pavel. Piotr is very nervous. Bazarov is calm and seated. Pavel enters, walking rapidly. He has a pistol case under his arm.

Pavel

I beg your pardon for keeping you waiting. I had to avoid waking the servants.

(He bows)

Bazarov

It doesn't matter. We only just arrived ourselves.

Pavel

So much the better. There's no one about to hinder us.

Bazarov

Let us proceed.

Pavel

You do not wish any further explanation?

Bazarov

No. I don't.

Pavel (offers the case)

Would you like to load?

Bazarov

You load. I will measure out the paces. One, two, three.

Piotr

Say what you like. I am going farther off.

Bazarov

Four, five. Go ahead, move off. Get behind a tree if you like. Six, seven, eight. Is that enough, or shall I add two more?

Pavel (who has loaded the weapons)

Do as you like.

Bazarov

Then we'll add two more. There's the barrier then.

Pavel

Will you be so good as to choose?

Bazarov

I will be so good.

(He picks one pistol)

Pavel

I am fighting in earnest.

Bazarov

No doubt.

(They back off about ten paces from the barrier and then approach)

Pavel

Are you ready?

Bazarov

Perfectly.

Pavel

We can approach each other.

(They walk towards the barrier. Pavel fires first and misses. Bazarov then fires, striking Pavel in the leg.)

Bazarov

Are you wounded?

Pavel

You have the right to a second shot.

Bazarov

Some other time.

(Pavel begins to fall and Bazarov catches him)

Pavel

No. Thank you. I need no one's help.

Bazarov

I am no longer a duelist, but a doctor. I'd better have a look at it. Piotr, come here.

(Piotr has fled and Pavel Petrovitch faints. Bazarov lays him on the grass and begins to treat him.)

Bazarov

What delicate skin!

Piotr (returning)

Is he dead?

Bazarov

The bone's not touched. The ball didn't go deep. Get some water quick, and he'll outlive us yet.

(Piotr stands transfixed, stupefied)

Go for water. Imbecile.

Pavel

No need. A momentary vertigo. Help me to sit up. I can walk back home.

(Chuckling)

He does look like an imbecile.

Bazarov

Let me bind your leg. But, I must first revivify this corpse.

(He shakes Piotr)

Now, get on home and say nothing.

(Piotr runs off)

Pavel

The duel, if you consent, shall not be renewed. You have behaved honorably, today, today—observe.

Bazarov

There's no need to recall the past, and I intend to be off without delay.

(Binding the wound)

I brought some bandages with me. Your wound is not serious, but it's best to stop the bleeding.

Pavel

At any rate there will be no scandal and for that I am thankful.

Bazarov

Have I bound up your leg too tight?

Pavel

No, not at all, it's capital. There's no deceiving my brother, we shall have to tell him we quarreled over politics.

Bazarov

Very good. You can say I insulted all anglophiles.

Pavel

That will do perfectly.

(Pause)

Look what that fool, Piotr, has done. Here comes my brother in a sprint.

Nicolai (enters, agitated)

What does this mean, Mr. Bazarov? What is this?

Pavel

Nothing. They have alarmed you for nothing. I have had a minor disagreement with Mr. Bazarov, and I have had to pay for it a little.

Nicolai

But, what in heavens name was it all about?

Pavel

Mr. Bazarov alluded disrespectfully to Sir Robert Peel and I called him out.

Nicolai

But, you're covered with blood!

Pavel

Well, do you suppose that I have ice water in my veins? But, bleeding is beneficial, isn't that so, doctor? Now, help me up and I shall walk home.

(Bazarov and Nicolai help Pavel to rise)

Nicolai

I must ask you to look after my brother till we get another doctor from town.

Bazarov

Of course. I shall leave whenever a competent surgeon arrives. I shall leave my address in case there's any fuss.

Pavel

There will be no fuss.

Nicolai

I shall manage that. I am very sorry your stay in my house should have such an end. It is the more distressing to me because of Arkady.

Bazarov (impatiently)

Don't trouble yourself. I shall drop in on Arkady to inform him. It will not destroy our friendship.

Pavel

You know, doctor, my opinion of your skill as a physician has changed.

Bazarov

Indeed?

Pavel

You're not half bad.

    (They help him out and there is a **SHORT CURTAIN**)

ACT IV
SCENE 11

Anna Sergeyevna's garden.

Enter Arkady.

Arkady (hesitating)

Well, there's no turning back now.

Katya (seeing him)

It's you!

(She is genuinely delighted)

Anna, Anna! Arkady Nicolaievitch is back.

(Anna enters)

Anna

Welcome back, runaway! Where did you find him, Katya?

Arkady

I have brought you something, Anna Sergeyevna which you

certainly didn't expect.

Anna

You have brought yourself, that's better than anything. And, where is Mr. Bazarov?

Arkady

He's still with my father. He has work to do.

Anna (disappointed)

Oh, such devotion to duty is a noble trait, I suppose. Katya, entertain our guest. I will return at lunch.

(Anna exits)

Katya

Well, so, you are here.

Arkady

I'm here.

Katya

And, alone. How courageous. Yes, I thought you went nowhere without Bazarov

Arkady

You see, however.

Katya

Have you shaken yourself free, or are you still under his influence, like my sister?

Arkady

I see you don't like him.

Katya

I have no opinion about him.

Arkady

Katerina Sergeyevna, that's impossible. There's no escaping it.

Katya

Very well. I don't like him, then. Or rather, I should say he's not my type. And, I think he's not your type, either.

Arkady

Really? I'm very fond of him.

Katya

But, he's a wild animal and we are tame.

Arkady

Am I tame, too?

Katya

Uh-huh.

Arkady

That's really an insult.

Katya

You want to be a beast, then?

Arkady

Not a beast, but strong, full of force and power.

Katya

It's no use wanting to be that way. You either are or you're not. Bazarov doesn't want to be that way, he simply is.

Arkady

You think your sister is still under his influence?

Katya

Yes. But, no one can keep the upper hand over her for long.

Arkady

Why?

Katya (slowly)

She values her independence a great deal.

Arkady

Who doesn't?

Katya

But, what good is it?

Arkady

Confess that you are a little afraid of her.

Katya

Of whom?

Arkady

Your sister.

Katya

And, how about you?

Arkady

Without a doubt.

Katya

My sister is very well disposed to you right now. Much more so than when you first came. Really. You haven't noticed it?

Arkady

But, why?

Katya

I have no intention of telling you.

Arkady

You are obstinate.

Katya

Very observant. Does that irritate you?

Arkady

No. I am wondering how you have come to be so observant. You are so shy, so reserved. You keep everyone at a distance.

Katya

Do I? But, I do not wish to keep everyone, (she speaks significantly) at a distance. I make exceptions.

Arkady

You are very kind.

Katya

It's my custom

Arkady

You know, you're just as independent as your sister? But, more reserved.

Katya (irritated)

Don't compare me with my sister, please. You seem to forget my sister is beautiful, clever—

Arkady

Katerina, let me tell you. I put you above you sister in every way.

Katya

Do you? I shall tell you something now. You can have your way with her.

Arkady

Katerina, what are you saying?

Katya

Exactly what I mean. You can have her. But you can't have me like that. Now, what do you say?

Arkady

As I said before. I place you above her, in all ways.

Katya

I rather thought you would change your tune. You could be her lover, you know. Seriously. She's had many. It's no secret. Everyone knows. Only poor Bazarov failed to attain his desire, because he wouldn't submit to her. Now she misses him, and is ready to console herself with you. As a surrogate. It's her way of being close to him.

Arkady

What you say is appalling.

Katya

Why don't you run to her?

Arkady

Because I love you.

(The enormity of his words terrifies him and he runs off)

(Anna returns)

Anna

Alone? I though you were with Arkady?

Katya

He went off.

Anna

You haven't been quarrelling, I hope?

(She puts her hand on Katya's chin)

Katya

No.

(Quietly removing her sister's hand)

Anna

How solemn you are. I was going to suggest taking a walk. He's always asking to do that.

Katya

Is he?

Anna

He's very nice. Don't you think?

Katya

Very

Anna

Shall we walk?

Katya

All right.

(They go off)

(A servant enters with Bazarov)

Servant

I though I should find him here, Sir. Shall I announce you to Anna Sergeyevna?

Bazarov

No. Just find him. I'll wait.

(A moment goes by. Bazarov fidgets. The servant returns with Arkady)

Arkady

This is unexpected. What good luck brought you? I suppose everything is all right at home? No one sick?

Bazarov

Everything's all right, but not everyone's well. Sit down. I'll tell you about it. Your Uncle found it necessary to challenge me yesterday.

Arkady

Good heavens! You didn't accept?

Bazarov

Unfortunately, I couldn't refuse. You see, my dear fellow, what comes of keeping company with feudal types. You turn into a feudal type yourself.

Arkady

But, is he hurt?

Bazarov

Yes. But, not badly. A wound in the thigh. He'll be all right.

Arkady

But, what was the cause of the quarrel?

Bazarov

I'm not sure, exactly. As you know, he's no great admirer of mine. Besides, he's rather peevish. Anyway, he got off lightly.

Arkady

I'm sorry it turned out like this.

Bazarov

Don't worry. I'm not troubled. It was a useless piece of foolery. I decided, however, to return to my father's, and I turned in here to see what I'm giving up.

Arkady

I hope you're not giving me up.

Bazarov

Would that trouble you? It strikes me you have given me up already. Your affair with Anna Sergeyevna must be getting on well.

Arkady

What affair?

Bazarov

Don't pretend you didn't come here on her account, or that

you're not in love with her. Or, are you just being discreet?

Arkady

You know, I've always been open with you. You're making a mistake.

Bazarov

Hmm, but, it's a matter of indifference to me. As for you and me, we're tired of each other.

Arkady

Eugeny!

Bazarov

Hell, there's no great harm in that. It's life. By the way, I forgot to tell them to hold the horses.

Arkady

But, Anna Sergeyevna will certainly wish to see you.

Bazarov

You're mistaken there.

Arkady

On the contrary. Besides, you know very well, you came intending to see her.

Bazarov

Perhaps. But, I've lost the nerve. Anyway, she won't care to see me.

(Anna Sergeyevna enters)

Anna

On the contrary, I most certainly do. Arkady, Katya is waiting for you.

(Arkady rises and leaves)

Anna

So, you're back.

Bazarov

Before everything, I must set your mind at rest, I came to my senses long ago.

(Anna receives this speech with mixed emotions. On the one hand, she is relieved that there will be no "scene," one with which, she secretly acknowledges to herself, she might not be able to cope. On the other hand, she is not too pleased that Bazarov has freed himself of her spell. Eventually, she concludes he has not, and her good humor returns.)

Anna

Let bygones be bygones. I was to blame for flirting. Let us be friends as before. That was a dream, wasn't it? And who remembers dreams?

Bazarov

Who remembers them? Love is just an imaginary feeling.

Anna

How true. I had a fit of depression. I even made plans to go abroad. Then it passed off. Now, I can resume my old part.

Bazarov

What part is that?

Anna

That of the guardian to Katya.

(Pause)

You know, I have never quite understood your friendship for Arkady. I thought him rather dull. But, I think, now, he is clever. And he's young above all!

Bazarov

Is he still shy with you?

Anna

Was he shy? Perhaps. I hadn't noticed.

Bazarov

It can hardly be any secret to you that he was in love with you.

Anna

What? Arkady, too?

Bazarov

You're hardly lacking in perception.

Anna

You are mistaken.

Bazarov

I don't think so. Let's walk.

(Bazarov and Anna go out. Arkady and Katya enter from another direction.)

Arkady

Katerina Sergeyevna, there is one very important subject we have not talked about.

Katya

Really?

Arkady

You!

Katya

Me?

Arkady

I am not the wretched self-conscious boy I was when I first came here. I want to be useful. Up till recently, I did not understand myself. I hope you understand me.

(Katya does understand him quite well, but, she is much to clever to say so)

Katya

I haven't the foggiest.

Arkady (agitated)

I think it the duty of everyone to be open with those people who are, who are, so I—

(Katya isn't helping a bit, she looks at her shoes)

I foresee, I shall surprise you. I am trying, to say—

(Anna and Bazarov have entered the garden without seeing Katya and Arkady. Arkady falls silent.)

Anna

You and I made a mistake, we are both past our first youth. I, especially so, we are both, why affect not to know it, clever, at first we interested each other, and then...

Bazarov

Them, I grew stale.

Anna

You know that was not the cause of our misunderstanding. We are too much alike. Now, Arkady—

Bazarov (grimly)

Do you want him?

Anna

Shh. You say he is not indifferent to me. I know I'm older, but, frankly, he's charming.

Bazarov (in a steady, but choking voice)

The word "fascination" is most frequently employed in such cases.

Anna

He's just like a brother to Katya. Perhaps, I ought not to have allowed such intimacy between them.

Bazarov (archly)

That caution is, no doubt, prompted by your feelings as a sister.

Anna

Of course. It's strange how I can confide in you. I'm afraid of you. But, I trust you, because you are so good.

Bazarov

I am not in the least good. And your confidences are like laying a wreath of flowers on a corpse.

(Bazarov and Anna disappear)

Arkady

Katerina Sergeyevna, I love you—no one but you. I ask for your hand, Surely, you must have known. Say one word.

Katya

Yes.

Arkady

You believe me?

Katya

Yes.

Arkady

Katya, Katya.

(They embrace)

(Bazarov and Anna have returned)

Bazarov

So, that's how it is? Well, I'm damned.

Anna

The younger generation have grown awfully sly.

Bazarov

In any event, it's time for me to go.

Anna

Don't go. It's exciting talking to you. Stay.

Bazarov

I thank you for the flattering opinion of my conversational talents. I'm a poor man, but I don't take charity. Goodbye.

Anna

I am certain we will see each other again.

(Bazarov leaves)

(Anna approaches Katya and Arkady, who separate in surprise)

Anna

Children, what do you say? Is love simply an imaginary feeling?

(They stare at her flabbergasted)

SHORT CURTAIN

ACT V
SCENE 12

Bazarov's parents' home again.

Bazarov is reading one of his father's medical books. He seems rather nervous. Old Bazazov tiptoes in and watches him. Bazarov becomes aware of it and slams the book down.

Bazarov

Why do you always seem to be walking round me on tiptoe? That way's worse than the old one!

(Bazarov gets up and walks out through the door to the porch)

Old Bazarov

There, there, I meant nothing. You shall forget me completely.

(But Bazarov has gone. Madame Bazarov enters from the living quarters.)

Madame Bazarov

If you could only find out, darling, what Enyusha would like for dinner today.

Old Bazarov

But, why don't you ask him yourself?

Madame Bazarov

Oh, he will get sick of me.

(Pause)

Enyusha's breaking my heart. He's always so silent and sorrowful. If only he'd let me put an amulet on his neck, that would cure his melancholy. If only he'd abuse us like he used to.

Old Bazarov

I think he's getting better. How he gave it to me just now. It was splendid.

Madame Bazarov

I know. But, it's so hard.

(She rushes back into the living quarters)

(Old Bazarov sits down and looks at the medical book his son was reading)

Old Bazarov

Hmm. I wonder why he was interested in this.

(Bazarov returns)

Bazarov

Dad, have you any caustic?

Old Bazarov

Yes. What do you want it for?

Bazarov

I need it for a cut.

Old Bazarov

For whom?

Bazarov

For myself.

Old Bazarov

What kind of cut is it?

Bazarov

I got it dissecting that peasant they brought in with typhus.

Old Bazarov

For God's sake, let me do it myself.

(Old Bazarov runs out and returns quickly with a bottle of caustic. He examines his son's hand with great agitation.)

Bazarov

What a devoted practitioner.

Old Bazarov

Don't joke. Show me your finger. The cut is not a large one. Does it hurt?

Bazarov

Press harder.

Old Bazarov

Perhaps, we had better burn it with a hot iron.

Bazarov

That should have been done sooner. Even now the caustic is useless, really. If I've taken the infection it's really too late.

Old Bazarov

How long ago?

Bazarov

More than four hours ago.

Old Bazarov

Why did you wait so long?

Bazarov

The village is quite a ways. And the village doctor had no caustic.

Old Bazarov

What?

Bazarov

You should have seen his lancets.

Old Bazarov

May I feel your pulse?

Bazarov

It's unnecessary. I'm feverish.

Old Bazarov

Has there been any shivering?

Bazarov

Yes, there has been shivering.

Old Bazarov

Perhaps, you have caught cold.

Bazarov (wryly)

Undoubtedly.

(Pause)

Dad, I'm in a bad way. I've got the infection, and in a few days, you'll have to bury me.

Old Bazarov

Nonsense. It's a coincidence. You've got a cold.

Bazarov

Hush! A doctor can't be allowed to talk like that. There's every symptom of an infection.

Old Bazarov

Even supposing—

Bazarov

Blood poisoning.

Old Bazarov

Very well, as you like, we'll cure you.

Bazarov

That's humbug. There's no cure. I didn't expect to die so soon. Most unpleasant. Most unpleasant. You and mother are deeply religious, it will be easier for you. For me, there is no consolation.

Old Bazarov

I shall rebel. I shall rebel.

Bazarov

Have you ever met people with blood poisoning who have not made off straight to the promised land? Poor mother. What will she do with her beet soup?

Old Bazarov (crying)

I shall rebel. I shall rebel. Where is God's justice?

Bazarov

Don't whimper, Dad. If Christianity is no help, be a philosopher. Didn't you always boast you were a philosopher?

Old Bazarov

What, me a philosopher?

Bazarov

What I dread most is losing my wits.

Old Bazarov

My son. My dear son.

Bazarov

Tomorrow, or the next day, my brain will send in its resignation. I'm not sure even now if I'm completely in command of myself. Am I? Do I sound all right?

Old Bazarov

Yes, yes, perfectly.

Bazarov

All the better. I want you to send—

Old Bazarov

For a doctor? At once. At once.

Bazarov

No, to—

Old Bazarov

To Arkady?

Bazarov

Let him be. No, to Madame Odinstov. Anna Sergeyevna. Say, send her my greetings. Tell her I am dying. That's all.

Old Bazarov

I will do it. I will do it.

Bazarov

Good. I should like it to go today. It's the only chance there is of her receiving it before—

Old Bazarov

At once.

Bazarov

I want to lie down, father. I feel dizzy. You break it to mother. I'm not up to that.

(Bazarov goes out)

Old Bazarov

If he dies, I shall rebel!

(He waves his fist to heaven)

SHORT CURTAIN

ACT V
SCENE 13

Same scene, two days later.

Bazarov is propped up in a chaise lounge covered with blankets. He is dying and feverish, but he refuses to give in. Old Bazarov is watching him.

Bazarov

(a+b) times (a+b) equals a2+2ab+b2. 10 take away 2 plus eight is 16.

Old Bazarov

Enyusha!

(He wants to say something, but can't)

Bazarov

I can still reason, Dad.

Old Bazarov

Eugeny, please God, you will get well, but to comfort your mother, (he hesitates) and me too. Perform the duty of a

Christian! You don't know how hard it is for me to say this to you, but, it would be worse if...think a little. For your mother.

Bazarov

I am not a Christian. However, if Father Alexey will perform the rites with that understanding, I will not refuse.

Old Bazarov

I will send, immediately.

Bazarov

There's no hurry. I shall last a while yet.

Old Bazarov

Eugeny, I beg—

Bazarov

Did you send to Anna Sergeyevna?

Old Bazarov

To be sure, I did.

Bazarov

If she were coming, she'd have come by now.

(There is a commotion at the door. Old Bazarov goes to the door. Anna's voice: I am Madame Odinstov. I have brought a doctor with me. Are you his father? Anna enters with a German doctor at her side.)

Old Bazarov

Benefactress.

German Doctor

Wo ist der Kranke?

Old Bazarov

Here, here, follow me.

(Bazarov sits straight up)

Bazarov

I want to see her.

Old Bazarov

But, first the consultation.

Bazarov

No. The consultation afterwards.

Old Bazarov

But—

Bazarov

I insist. Leave us alone.

German Doctor (whispering)

I can tell from this distance, it is hopeless. Notice his shining eyes. It's a sure sign.

(He and Old Bazarov go out)

Komm! You can give me his symptoms while they talk.

(Anna and Bazarov are left face to face)

Bazarov

Thanks. I didn't expect this.

Anna

I hope—

(She is dismayed)

Bazarov

Ah, Anna Sergeyevna, let us speak the truth. It's all over with me. So far, I'm not afraid, but delirium is coming. I've fought it off till now. But, I can't hold out much longer. Well, what I had to say to you. I love you. You didn't want to hear it before. It disturbed your peace of mind. But, now, it cannot upset you.

Anna (half to herself)

It upsets me, Eugeny. It upsets me.

Bazarov

Never mind. Don't be uneasy. Don't come too close.

(Anna goes directly to him)

Ah, you are brave. How lovely you are, too. Make the most of life while there is time. I frittered away my time. I thought I was a giant. There were problems to solve and things to be smashed. And now the problem is for this giant to die decently. But, I'm not going to turn tail. You will forget me. My father will tell you what a man Russia is losing. That's nonsense. Russia doesn't need me. But, don't contradict the Old Buzzard. And be kind to mother. It's clear, I wasn't needed. Who is needed?

Anna

Don't agitate yourself so much.

Bazarov

What difference? My cup is full. You have come. I'm starting to get mixed up.

Anna

Lie back. Rest. I shall be here.

Bazarov

Tailors are needed. Butchers are needed.

(He falls asleep)

(Anna waits a moment. Old Bazarov and the German Doctor return)

Old Bazarov

Can we have a look at him?

Anna

He's asleep.

German Doctor

He's dead.

Anna

No. No. He can't be. I had so much to say to him.

German Doctor

Tot.

(Anna weeps)

Old Bazarov

I said I would rebel. And, I rebel. I rebel.

(He waves his hands wildly and begins smashing things)

(Madame Bazarov enters and folds her husband in her chubby arms)

CURTAIN

ACT V
SCENE 14

Pavel Petrovitch's room.

Fenitchka comes in with a cup of tea for Pavel, who is lying in a chaise lounge with a blanket up to his waist. Fenitchka is about to rush out.

Pavel

Where are you going in such a hurry, Fedosya Nikolaevna? Are you busy?

Fenitchka

No.

(She wants to get away, but can think of nothing better than:)

I have to pour tea.

Pavel

Dunyasha can manage. Sit a little with a poor invalid. I want to have a little talk with you.

(Fenitchka sits on the edge of a chair, but says nothing)

Listen. I've wanted to ask you something for a long time. I've noticed, you seem to be afraid of me. Are you?

Fenitchka

Me?

Pavel

You. You never look at me—as though you felt guilty about something.

Fenitchka

What should I feel guilty about?

Pavel

I don't know. Have you wronged someone? Not me, surely. Who, my brother? But you love him, don't you?

Fenitchka

I love him.

Pavel

With all your heart?

Fenitchka

With all my heart.

Pavel

Truly? Look at me, Fenitchka. It's a great sin to lie.

Fenitchka

I am not lying.

Pavel

You wouldn't cheat on him?

Fenitchka

Heavens, no. As God is my witness.

Pavel

What about that doctor fellow?

Fenitchka

How can you say such things?

Pavel

You know I saw.

Fenitchka

What did you see?

Pavel

When you were picking flowers.

Fenitchka

How am I to blame for that?

Pavel

You were innocent? Are you sure?

Fenitchka

Very sure. I love Nicolai Petrovitch. Mr. Bazarov was very nice, but he shouldn't have done that. It was unfair, and I couldn't say anything.

(Pavel suddenly takes her hand and presses it)

Pavel (excitedly)

Love him. Love my brother. Don't give him up for anyone in the world. There is nothing more terrible in the world than to love and not be loved. Never leave my brother.

(Fenitchka doesn't know what to make of Pavel. He still frightens her. Nicolai enters carrying the baby. Fenitchka runs to him and embraces him.)

Nicolai

What's the matter? You don't feel worse?

Pavel

On the contrary. Never better.

(Fenitchka runs out with the baby)

Nicolai

You were in a great hurry to move on the sofa. I was bringing my young hero to see you. Now, why did she take him off?

What's going on?

Pavel

Brother!

Nicolai

Eh—

Pavel

Brother, give me your solemn word of honor you will carry out my one request.

Nicolai

What request?

Pavel

I have been thinking a great deal. It is very important. Brother, do your duty. Put an end to this scandal.

Nicolai (aghast)

You want me to send her away?

Pavel (earnestly)

Marry Fenitchka. She loves you. She is the mother of your son.

Nicolai

But, it is only out of respect for you that I haven't married her all this time. I thought you opposed such misalliances.

Pavel

You were wrong to pay any attention to my views, they're snobbish and old hat. Bazarov was right, you know. I'm just an old aristocratic snob.

Nicolai

That reminds me, Bazarov is dead.

Pavel

What? But, he is so young and vigorous.

Nicolai

He contracted blood poisoning doing an autopsy.

Pavel

I knew no good would come from all his dissections. It may surprise you, but I am very sorry to hear it.

Nicolai

Indeed? Arkady is shattered, of course. But, with your views, I thought—

Pavel

You were right about him. He had something. Energy. Honesty. He meant well. I still don't doubt that the road to hell would be paved with his good intentions and that we are destined to fight. Still, he was a worthy opponent.

Nicolai

What I'm afraid of is that there will be more like him.

Pavel

If that day comes, our country will be torn apart.

Nicolai

Hmm.

CURTAIN

ABOUT THE AUTHOR

Frank J. Morlock has written and translated many plays since retiring from the legal profession in 1992. His translations have also appeared on Project Gutenberg, the Alexandre Dumas Père web page, Literature in the Age of Napoléon, Infinite Artistries.com, and Munsey's (formerly Blackmask). In 2006 he received an award from the North American Jules Verne Society for his translations of Verne's plays. He lives and works in México.

www.ingramcontent.com/pod-product-compliance
Lightning Source LLC
LaVergne TN
LVHW041620070426
835507LV00008B/362